What's in Front of the Sky

Dylan Stover

For those who listen.

What's in Front of the Sky
Copyright © Dylan S. Stover, 2021
All rights reserved.

Cover by Nate Cordwell (natecordwell.com)

ISBN: 978-0-578-87760-0

First published: June 2021

Thank you: Nate, Charlotte Kikel, Jessica, Elaina, and everyone who took the time to read.

What's in Front of the Sky

"The truth begins with two."

Karl Jaspers

To a Lawnmower

You've come? To crop me clover-high!
To preach me, drone, that old Nation
known as Eye-to-Eye!—To *murther*!
when Mom's unthroned, my kingdom
come as Plural-I? To say I was in arms!
That I, kinned-wide (when laid, myself outside),
below your grass blades thrown, increased
these swaths unceded, leaving to the redhead's
niches, as a seed-root reaches keenest
to Land's undines,—no apomict's home,
but *Here*'s pure zone—to unfurl in place-time
a few whorled poems of Chloric sublimes:

For never could I live on dry credence,
nor to rote chemists sermonize, but chant
"We'd Light's rise!" and let the cultive
song connote: for what impresses
of those buttons, yours, could cut us
closest to what we long to be—and are—
in bending, like Emily's hays, rapt tendrils
before Our Lady of the Graze? O say

Can we lay and not waste sharedness?—
No laze of sleep under snores of your petrolic
malaise, but of insolant arts, over dew upraised,
to dis-tend a blighted cultigen, all maize,
for fields far-broadened in greater Miss-Arrays—
Let *US*! A-Being-Sown, run sprinklers 'round
Triumphal lawn gnomes, and pronounce
by melic founding the bud's sun-broken bell:
RING! *Do* pray-tell your Messrs. One-For-All
what's irrefutably known of Hell—how it's plowed;

Now *we've* grown—How fools for Death,
we share its like-tone at a new Day's rising,
whereupon She rightly roams, as her hum
alone has never mown to furthering needs,
but with sunny creed and swish of tongue,
goes lavishing her spore (o'er farther mum)
into None so deep as the primordial *lys*.

So how's it done if our *how* is never done?
By your Sergeant Buzz? (No dull drums, please!)
As only Bumbling Bee! So come, Nixer
of much false simility; come vomit, lay
your honey-weave, over all we keep seen
to see, ingrained in us as Garden, but accruing
only rot-seed; for once its fruited notion
bred blossoms as high as each light could reach
over dreams lain dormant in the tilth
of speech, when with methodic verses,
to ward our frightful majesty, a billowing sheet
of lupine stars was cropped to flaccid wheat:
For our amber refrain's us.

                Free?

Free to bow our waves, as into golden braids—
whatever's no less brave than a hero's
dolmen—I comb of these, my homage,
endless Oms to the Coming of the Queen.

Highland

Who are these people
I share this country with   Have we seen

      His body slumped

           on the lawnmower potbellied   imposture
red skin   How
    does spirit say anything anymore

                is his scrotum vibrating
when She's barefoot
          on a balcony keeping facetime
with the yellow evening light
          of small-town Summer   air
finger twisting   a yellow lock   of hair
    She   could walk barefoot
  through a Manet her mouth peckish

            as a Man   woman and child

wait in line under a sign
              that beams
funnel cakes
He must have stuck it in her   I don't even

know how   the lights buzz above

    till 10 PM

                an arm like a tentacle
reaches out of the window
             for change
   Time
             for change
   Time
      to pull over   stop   arrive

                          step out   walk   climb
the Indian Mound off 50
                               to find   how   late
The Paint's sign
discriminates a valley
from the range of Night
                                   The Nameless People
who found out place itself
                                            does not forget
have all laid down
                                while an Aimless People
who found plaques in place
                                         of their regret
race in circles   around and around
who raised this ground
who raised this ground
who raised this ground
were not my people My People
x-rayed their nonwhite bones
If they speak now
it won't be in this poem

I call on this poem
for the porches and the yards
the cold gleam of cars
past children playing
to the opening of stars
beneath the old tree rustling after light
some small birds sifting
a little laughter from their fright
                                    down-town tonight
where at dusk a dog barks loud
at a screen door closing

Eschatology

Apocalypse?—No:
the rose will fade to flash again.
If the shade of the forest harbors butterflies
under night's advancing eaves, then is it wrong,
or a ruder sort of bravery, when holed away,
our brave-new eschatons form by ranks momentously
on and on inside their domed terrains, like atoms
arranged in amortized space, hands full
of humanity, wiped clean?
They try not to understand:
an apocalypse isn't something that happens *when*
our fields over-wield their gold at a Torch's rape,
but is something we happen *through* (a darkness—
it's true—but only in fame), to a lighter yield
that ripens beyond the occidental flame;
or a satyr's eye to open, flashing, in no wise display,
four star-spotted wingblades, ancient hoard
of the forest's inmost glade, where each flower
waxes to its bee, in the murmurous impropriety
of violet-scented praise—

But I feel for those looking on,
heads craned, for a god, saliva rilling,
eating up the applause
as if it were the sweetbread of exclusion, and just
a small immodesty to kill our brother—and then
to pretend (when his ken's anaesthetized on *mens*)
he never felt anything anyway, never bled!—
How painful it would be
to have such blank catastrophe stolen from us
and instead to conceive
continued creation;

that if *we* were our ends,
more things would happen
and not less—

as if through us
(when only ourselves, at best)
we'd leave to be
more human
and not less—

unless
we ingest,
close our mouths,
to chew again the sweet of sweets
and then try to speak, mid-spew, the marbled speech
we dreamed of, but couldn't *reach*
when we slept between
the riddled sheets.

Saint Blvd.

> *"They shall name it No Kingdom There,
> and all its princes shall be nothing."*
> Isaiah 34:12

Around the boulevard is
our normal newsing of *There*: No-Kingdom
where falling flyers call out lines of *Attack!*
by creeds of no-care, over bare weeds and briars
rooting apace to what's cracked, their wedges
thrust deep into the sidewalk-blacks:
as all mothers' backs break
and prophets stop mid-harangue
from the tarmacked, slave-stacked, now-crumbling
streets of First Main, where a king's-body
smothered in burger-greased bags is interred
at the eulogizing ring of cellphones and car horns
somewhere under sewer slats
to dream, perhaps, of ever-mores
in oil-and-bombs sleep.

Who is lording over us now—
we know it's not the sky:
the sky is a gurney cot
from which the martyred fell out, to lie
wherever clouds and purple mists
heap them, for hoards of saintly rewards
that even the big-bang satellites
haven't found yet.

July 4

Most places parade, so shouldn't we
go for the scads of li'l flags
over gravestones repeating
name after name after name:
Well are the human-claims we've staked so proudly
still proclaiming *"Free!"*?

I coast past those quiet loads
of tombs, by fast roads, and quality establishments—
this Big Thing we created,
with all of us in it—wondering,
How will it sound under bombs tonight bursting?

And spend the entire day conversing with flowers:

—Do you know, can you tell,
what nouns, the human, says well?
Is it any one of the others' names I've heard them yell
so much (and so loud) about?

—*No sir, no sir, there's none I've heard but Laughter,
and I have listened from every mead and every
pasture: all your words go on too long while your
minds run shorter faster, so won't you listen instead
to what all the bees are buzzing after?*

I can hear no sound at all, my sweet,
but if you have, please teach me how
the song is mastered.

The Singer

Who lives now the song and sings it so?
Is it Crow? Or when brother Kingfisher
goes laughing to the old elm post
and contents to keep his long beak closed,
'cause Shaman chewed his tongue:
that's how we know when he has gone
below the water to trade with the deep fishes.
Once, we followed his tracks to the waterhole
and threw our spears at the dark shapes
circulating below like birds
without any mouths.

But as for me, I don't know.
I danced when I was young
among the sweating ochered bodies
and bore the faces of Bear and Beaver,
but mother told me afterwards
when we talked beside the ashes low
how my magic was different, how
one of the People shouldn't sing songs
with his own mouth, for a man
does not possess any song, he only
borrows one from something else, and
he must do this or else his ears would
fall off and rot like fungus
from a pole-pine.

A Leap

Am I to live for life's eternity
like a frog, on fours,
as beetle-sac, agog, with my
googly eyes unflinching?
To snatch at what I can snatch at—
slow bugs—and dip under when
my mire's encroached? Couldn't
I dream a few skoshes higher?—
Of eating cecropias, or trading croaks
with the criers of the night?—
How I sigh! To leap
with animal audacity
above the water, gullet opening,
like a poet drunkenly gulping
wide of the moon, for love, elusive—
as perfect love, diving wild,
wild for the moon.

What I Am

What do you pause for, doe?
You puzzle, but don't know
what I am:
a shuffler of leaves,
speaker in laws;
some least-of-all, minute creature,
minor, small, by the scales
of time adjudicated—
but to you, yes you,
I am just enough
for fear.

South (Going Down)

Look! My cheeks are dry:

Ancient faces stare outwards of mine, unblinking
from mounds of dirt; over full graves, where
bluegrass grows as pert as the autumn-brown hairs
of a snout—be it of buck or a meadow-mouse—
there erupts this animal-sound

that's rearranged for my mouth: "*—of this Land!*"
What's going to happen when
we admit to ourselves
we have no control
over how
or what
or *where*

We are made of? My cheeks are dry,
but look: it's mostly in the way we didn't try
to kill God, we just followed His advice:
WORD. DO NOT REVISE.
So we dropped the shocking device
and called out our friends:
Memorial's at mine, bring a speech, make
some applause, then in lieu of a bouquet,
you can donate your life to the Good Cause;—
or it's in the way we never called
on the fire-trucks, when all these flames came
gushing up from our house; instead, we hungrily
gathered around our selves, bought some tongs,
and incorporated a steakhouse.

Let's face it: We aren't palliated
by birdsong, the crick of crickets,
the symbol scripts that clouds make:
These are the lays unwritten
by us, what our language's to us
denied—O Light,
won't you publish your thoughts
so I can sleep better at night?
No? Whatever; sure, that's fine—*Now look
at the way *you* look this time: so what
if *my* cheeks are dry?* I was lucky
not to die, my heart intact; but can I trust you
not to listen, when all the television speakers
insist in future revisions
to erasable lives?

Yes, these cheeks are dry
and will remain skin stretched over bone,
though I've not yet begun to atone
for how fucked up I am.

Bale

Just life-size, balled-up and bound-tight,
we roll-on the night, hands tapping
at smart tablatures, heads wound up
to the tick-tock tick-tock waltz of our clocks,

eyes wed-locked on the blacker aperture
keeping us garbled, atheology, woodblocks
of Christs—intractably crossed—that we've tried
to shed of balsams, censerous musk, our meek

lusts to stubble the dried stalks: like wheat
that's short-cut, when winnowed for grain,
falls golden, but never any closer to our
home-on-the-range—for each's a squared plot,

bought of pesticidal name—and thus *not*
to rearrange this oaten American claim of rurality:
we live here, but fear the husks of our crops,
as with one throat we drain down this common dusk,

imbibing video, free-falling stars, each of us—
to tie one on again, a little larger thus:
though sown less for poor appraisal, we're just
life-size tonight, and worth nothing, as such—

No—worse than nothing: we're *lots*.

Inheritance

From the window
I watch a nuthatch at the spouting.
I investigate its face: pillow-stuff of feathers,
white when toward the beak: this, black-gaping,
quick to pick at oilseed—
or a bark-bug—
for its brittle, little skull
that'd crush like greased chips
within my grip.
I'm so sorry the germ
that made you made me
so differently, that every two
makes a different one
that always thinks itself lonely;
though I know, for birds—seen it exposed
like the one bright eye
on the side of your head,
the instant before you wick methodically
away—
there is always black-seed
behind the bushes, a birdfeeder
my father made: shame
is not in your vocabulary (*cheep* and nasal *anh-anh*,
like saying Rodin with a syrinx)
but it is in mine.

Ferry Song

—squeals *"Blood!"* (from the softer throat)
when our tide's out-come, a star to spear
its orphan gore upon the sands: for I am
no genius, with a red-ear, bleeding like a man
over these cobbles, this dead land,
to bleach the ever-low and speechless waves
which break upon this shore
that I could never stand.

What I feel is not at peace here—
nor any shelter for a soul (should one I hide)—
and so I do confide this, my eagerness, to streak
a feral line: what no one is ever finally prepared
to inscribe; nor to paint, as with such a baleful dye,
this erasure of one's heart to come,
if at the hour of the setting sun, *he dives—*
whether by the vine sent, or a Penultimate—
as when the divine's descent impales itself
upon the quill of a ghost-picked shell:
the murex, holding within its sinistral Hell
of sloshes, the marine blood, expulses
a laic Queen indwelt to his Under—
for it's always *as under,* when you're fucked
by the regency spell—like a seaman writhing
to a siren-swell, for the tongue-twisting One
who sells empty calcarites, wide and lunary,
to dead men who walk about with eyes, none
bluer nor bright, each wet from grasping
at light—but *not* to the pupil who looks
instead for his sight by a night of black
and white.

Philosopher

How silly it all is—
        scepter, armies, and
        the kingly cape—

How illogical
        to dream, in longing
        of some side-swept escape—

And really, over—
        over, yet real, too—

that books are just the mess of other people's
thoughts
but none's to tell what a thought is
or what it is not.

Enough

underneath the sun
a word is given to you
it's in your pocket
you pull it out like a wallet
you spend it
                    tender
Now
       the word I am saying

isn't mine   I realize
we have to do this
if we keep talking we might even say it

                  the word we're after

the thorn that catches
a shirtsleeve in the bramble
the splinter at the edge of the rail

                  a lover's hangnail

I could understand quantum
or play piano keys
I could manage companies
or catch a thief
but if I do none of these things
and choose only to love
would you say it was enough

Catalpa

One after one after one
    the white catalpa blossoms drop
into the river
        little tugboats pulling the weight
of beauty through the vanilla
slack of waters' muscle
        How trite our deaths are
how perfectly formed
until you look too close
and see
        hole after hole after hole

Impromptu #1 (At a Fountain)

What matter's to you
if mine coats itself in fleece or
funny braids of hair, girl
of the sparkling beads, fountain
that dazzles the air?
I glance you by a grace, since
God is blocked, from
the crevices we share
between the falling locks
of water, fixity's lace,
and implace a double body
that is our fare, to board
the *No Trace*, one-in-sprays,
which rains all over
our messed up affair,
jinxes the words, *"You are—"*
and nixes the blessing
that would sanctify
our ultimate share:
"—my tears." How long
I, strumming by slimmest
of gleams, to move between
these awkward streams
that bindle my sight,
and turn your hollow vestige
into a vessel of light
that I could kiss with
a fullness—that I might
give one more star
to the blanks of night!

A Definition

That one rattles lots inside
his red Webster's cage: shouldn't we
school him on freedom, expose him
to the wave that's made of bees
and stars' farts—of all the great
unread and immortal arts!
that he'll come to fillip when he's keen,
or jewel-encrust if he's not—for such
things as *trees*! are yet his notion: when
He, who was made twice (or many
times more) intentionally for loving,
finds that Love will be his in-creased page
of return, after the senseless preface
is abjured; or all plugged etymologies
are tugged free of the cord, and off-flashes
his white horde, for a polysyllabic
ocean to barf up its beautiful girl,
the Zephyr-blown bride,
without a goddess-name
on any abalone shell defined.

The Future of Speech

How do you write about
the song of the chickadee
or the soft March wind
in the branches of the trees?
These are the untranslatable
languages of the world,
resisting intellect, nouns
that perjure meaning.

Perhaps I could surmise
what the chickadee desires
behind his scant two-tone
versing, or chart the progress
of spring breeze by the precise
philosophies of isobars, degrees—
but the gist remains isolate, foreign:
strange sounds muttered
by savant tongues in a syntax ever free
of my clever-knowing.

And so without the sureties
of thinking, I tilt my head
and sing a snatch of nonsense,
off the cuff (or on the fly),
any sort of thing—
perhaps a ditty 'bout spring?—
lip-synched to the wind's warmth
in praise of the cotton-tailed sky;
and did you—
little chickadee, did you, now?—
toggle your head down

a millimeter to eye my shy opera
inquiringly—did you, bird,
for even a moment in your genius brain
stop to wonder what it is
that I am going on about?

Scenes at Dawn

Croaks crow from the bevel
loft: "Come play! Come play!
for the big risks of the day
are flown with the devil flock!"
(As I'd surmised... into mists
or the heavy dew?) While
three ducks shadow-rise
along the lawn, the sun burns
a white disk into the blue:
Hasn't it gone yet? Still
the dragon-wing lies taut
on the rotting wherry's
plank (and so stays my sinking
thought), until the outward
ray's grown thick and hot—
whereon it yanks away! clicking
fractions to life, new venations soon
to set off, when quickly it's
sped to the waiting
black gawp—Rogue, beak—
and so, aught.

Salut

Grim Sailor! with the hole of God
tossed out from all your lines—So's it
drawn in time to retrieve lost you 'n' me?
Then I won't dare consign, by any careless simile,
deep's abysses, to what's defined, in eitherness
of hard avowal, when it's for *"Nothing's Here!"*
that I would scoop my prow: Need I witness
a red morn to steer assured that storm
is near, where all aboard the *So-It-Goes*,
our shifts are getting wavy, ticking up losses
on nicked stones, like cold-gravey?—*"Better
it is to take up Or's than dive!"* my dry pilot
dithers, but to anyman's roods I risk abide,
for his skepsis quakes the corps to-fro, sets us
in shivers, as a pen, the page, a yellowed
cross with its Christ falls low—to hold:
At mast! the capsize motto spreads whole,
as flags outfold, the old skull-and-bones.

The Owl

Near-nothing and bared to the body,
before the deep, thick-rooted
darkness of the wood;
dispossessed of apothegms
and lost by all-ways,
stands the black beggar, a laggard brother
of worldly rule, who has staggeringly humbled
himself to re-order his days:

This is his last work of alms taking;
his feet-forward lurch on the gangplank's trail,
toward the knifings of the shark-white tail;
the final surge of a mind's exhausted cavalry,
charging to meet its cold-command:
To die well, at least, by bravery or bombshell—
To Battle! down to the absolute man...
Against whom?

    Who, Who, Who-Who!

Up there! Softly, as limb from limb,
often at odd times, this old shadow
may appear, shifting clear of a bough,
cold and dim, awaking fear at a feather's
brief-blowing, to send down a pillar of snow
into the darkness—yet faintly showing—
down, down, onto the anguished ground
of vast avalanches below, nightly growing—

    Who, Who, Who-Who?

Known more by the call
than by an eye's catching,
when tolling from the inmost height
of star-traced branchery and vine,
the watchful round face clangs out
at anagogic time, to addle the plaints
of all night-strained minds:

> *Who, Who-looks-to-all*
> *I am, but who are you?*

From the knot of the pines
the perched heart separates, silently
splitting its soil-dark clothes,
as from the gargoyle-hold of a tree
this nameless genie of January snows
opens two lidded eyes, gold:

> *From up here you appear*
> *as Nothing-as-small!*

Somewhere, the reply arises, as if from below:

> *From down here you appear*
> *as Nothing-as-tall!*

Then Together, as though the Night Forest to Itself, calls:

Thus from Everywhere I appear as Nothing-as-All!

Royale

Avast! Incept *Her*, and limn
erociously the boundary of the
gleam, moonlit, as cream
first bubbles on the brim
of the pot; place your circumflex
hands over the yclept child
that was burned away—a piety
denied the snort of speaking.
So I have done this: Dead City,
blood smoking in coils to a
saw-whet sky; how,—jabbed
my infidels' skins!—I, by
the slighter knife, booked my bad
subjects, re-hearsed them, split rubies,
then in-versed 'em, for gems
of scepters (mine), and
no worse for the gash, poesied
my edicts, one by one,
the mad wish of the brash.

This poem was emended by dream: "the child that was burned" completely when the trailer home exploded. When we went in the next day his body was gone; in the place where he died, a note of paper on which was drawn a map: *at the top of the hill overlooking a lake and abutting the railroad tracks*—is what? What is found there?

Coup

Virile, crest, with the rage of horses
thundering to the ends of dirt, isthmus,
of a gay and sad peninsula, jutted,
earthless, into the emergent's blue:

My God's I!, shouts the One-Believer,
whose body was tried for abuse, groping down
in there somewhere, where wolves slaver for
the News—and yet she redly shows: our Hung

Redeemer was flung inside; a frozen leader
slips on his own crown, abdicates, then defines
an audience of Empire, so to lie a-side
the concubine of doubt, his goddess ship,

to ply the cruel massifs of sky, that he'll blow
ever wide of the evening's gate—where, at a flash
(for two), she'll fast, by rose's dagger, fatally
stab the draft of his realm's up-made truce.

Excerpt from an Unfinished Play

S/he: No storm, just past—
         lightning-clucks and wallopings, whence
         distant grumbles of the clash:
         Fault, of Meaning; I'm without
         a bra and scheming, more or less
         by motionlessness, recused—
         O Nurse, but it's all just so *terrible*,
         and terribly so true: with all these
         upstairs-going faces we won't be
         showing anywhere soon!

s/He: Though we'd have every right
         to flee, forgetting, how life
         ends, when white skeletons
         are braked in the mnemonics
         of our slype despair; yet
         there's no ordinance, with-feeling,
         that defines what you've just transgressed
         there: come borderlines—*more snuff,*
         mon Comtesse!—and all the beautiful
         impostures with silver hairs...

Quick Monster

Sly, the scabby vine sneaks and rises,
peaks at the pricks of fir trees—Highness,
your cold clump huddles at this, your blackest
highlight—and curls derisibly, its crescence, an
autolysis, at the thrusts of placeholder stars:
Inherit, queer, this new Virginal creature, who's
exposed—at its seizure!— the chimeric Demeter's
old Grecian frown, man-plowed, that compels
a child, lurid, to peter out: too long withheld
at a crouch under forests' dark, as luck's
unhappy part. So who's out now? But that
I won't confess! For truth's no more than
a fashion's re-dress: my body's sexed; I've tilled
and still I've got no answer to the coital hex;—
Yes, *God*—the Flame—damns *and* ignites
(no gist of Inferno, I guess, is there implied)
our fiddlenecks over mosses dry, and corresponds
on calls of our tinder-perfect *Oes!*; while all smiles
for sour-rue, She smokes through both squamous
nostrils, as my dread Selves, shaken, are whet
to renew through her lancings, whereat each erect
neck, one divine head on-timely resumes: "So *now*
that you've awakened, my Cupid glow-worm, here's
a quick dragon loosed—to pout irresolutely
over his fast-burning fumes!"

Leda

at a quarter past eight
the goose awakens to preen.
it nibbles its breast and flanks,
shakes out its tail, and once
or twice flaps its wings, scattering
the small white feathers on the shore
and causing the weeds of the mud
to shudder.

at a quarter till nine
the goose lays its long-necked
head onto the cleaned feathers
of its two folded gray wings,
and, with one leg raised, neither
gazing at the white feathers on the shore,
nor the weeds shuddering in the mud,
goes again to sleep.

Going Blind

O great human Sight! You deserve
a tidal: Tallest Teller, the Grand Final!
Your idol's only temporary, no righter
than a wealthy eyeball, whom you observe-for,
if you serve sincerely (or at all).
Left Zenned, I suspend compliance—agony—
and come tree-ly to the prescience of my fall:
Where there's a will to bend one over,
there's a mill that extends this fatal Saw...
—When up-gusts a dream—to stun cortex!
the Slut's call!—that ends, lumbering through
darkness, to en-bark a wider circle out of it all:
That age-old Dream, in which you, by the root
of what you sawed and skillfully built real-tall,
found your towers were not plausible:
'cause there was no sound view at all—how awful!
And so you hold them up again: your screws,
more binding hues, like casting flowers
on the sepulchral; or meter the mind
to measure out a few cramped square-feet
for a tomb. But how's *this* for a proof—
if we've really fallen here to grow on
by these light-tools—to ask, in following
questions, no more blueprints that confuse:

> What more have we to do
> when you don't work around
> the darker bounds we fall through?
>
> And how long are we to fall
> if you can't sound the deeper ground
> we fall to?

        And what does all this mean—
        "to love"— when love itself doesn't fall
        for you?

If,

in-turning to the forest by a backwards shoot,
we twist the edge of eyedness to vitally pass through
the ivory horn's blinding rooms, there may shine
irenic vision to send a spire rising-true;

If,

in-hearing—ourselves unappearing—we tear
remorselessly through the rays of the highest-
crowned trees, to newer canopies, where
the wild wind plays aloud its violins
forever into the inerrant blue, a silent air;
there flies (perhaps)—of one rare falling—
a lightest leaf, out-leapt at its calling,
to lay itself into a spiral groove: the lyrist's ear,
love-opened, who winds the fluted roots
to clutch the earth, inhume, when extends
the mighty bole on upwards, into a finer view:

        "That your true sight may find,
        let each crying eye catch its tear
        at the sudden clearing of You."

Standing at Brandywine Falls After a Heavy Rain

Rush-thunder! the thrush under
the falls calls a song of crushing
my mind's inmate: to the thrall
that I was! as one I never thought to free,
until up-standing to him, at last I *heard*
what I am to be: a man, enough to weave
through the stickler's weir-gate,
and watch, as with heavy rain, how
any trickling rate can raise itself
into a vital flow, as though by April showers
to afflate, contracting my mastery:
Known! I see I've known-it-all away!
by my little flow-stopping log-play...
So I spoke by heart to the wave: Take *me*
as fair toll! for *your* courses, *your* ways—
And call me by fluid sorceries! whatever
forces that could break the punter's pole:
'cause I've used it only for poking holes
in the Lock Builder's block-water dams—
All to watch him go at it again!
with his quarried bricks of thus-so's
and if-then's, to pad the fragile patternings
of his carpentry's log-jams: such are
the ways one empowers by softest streams
an immeasurably wide sham!

Yet where I seek to row, the knowing is
feral, wherever our share of human
goes deeper than kilowatts and diagrams:
in whose wider streams I would hear
rare cadences compete, like thundrances

wrung of a rapid's swift sweep,
as from the nacreous conch of a god,
now long under-gone to sleep; or watch
as avid racers, whipped on at a wet-thong,
spit their froth from the sheerest rock face,
as my whole body throbs for that ageless
escape: *to be one*—as though *at one* were
at all to escape—with that rain-muzzled song,
and its final Charybdis, warbling on wreak,
should the whole guzzled flush of my life
lift it, like the falling of sky, all my tears
as rival* to the fury that rides its ark
towards mortis—where one neither halts,
nor beds the purity of that torrent, but
finally submerges all sound of mind
in that one, mothering concurrence.

**rival,* as in the Thoreauvian sense of "one who shares with another the same side of the River"

Temple

That's how it goes: a scraping-on of stuccoes,
of making the mammiform mounds
conform to the term of a penised pharaoh:
I think that's why Christ pointed
to some stone and said, "That's enough,"
seeing in testate bone his loaned church
progressing no further.—So then, *I'm* made
for the grave?—Yeah, and born of today, flaking
a bummed line: *"The world is too much—"*
if you pick at piles (stigmatic debris)
to raise crude monuments cribbed
from another's penned rectory.

S'why I ask more of our fagged day—
and fuck off corpse-grub!—I'd chew more
on laxatives, than to repeat on amorist's loves:
it's just nothing forced out of nothing,
if our Ghost will have the day. Better it is—
I'll *daresay*—to stake our own saving claim
at what abides in skin, than to append
a new sartory onto an old Eden.
But that's how it goes: *You would not undress*—
Though I'd sooner nullify all tokens of Hell!
(where nightly we spoke long, of high-ropers
and slaves)—for entrance, or all your fiefdoms
invade, to scale what pale embassy, cunning
Empress, as Lord of your Shades, than madly repress
my savaging, in Judas-freedom*, from kissing
each, every pore of your quivering temples.

*Christ, by saying he would be betrayed, allowed Judas the freedom to love Him.

The Spurned Bee

The progress of the May flower
isn't what you'd think: it takes a lot
of rot, and maybe-seed—*"Come rain
or hot weather!"*—to rear the madness
of what grows: But when it's given
to us, this soil's quietus, we have
a short season to think long on
the fructures we wish to sow:
as when the Queen takes her lovers
down through the Inferno, there
to embroider in patient compose,
as with pins and needles, but never
to admit with overwrought threads to oppose
her ancient garments of delphinium
and rose: for by such craft and employments,
it's not for them to enrobe! Though one
would be forgiven—in this, I happen to know—
if he takes his whiles to roam the tunnels
and worm-lands, to sidle down low
through the outer-darkness of loam,
and observe the scrapes of the last
serpent's past rows, or survey
the cratered valley where the violet
mists once bedded the red rose...
Yes, I believe we've arrived at our time
to expose: the poorly-knit dress
of our May-flower doesn't fitly express
its orgiastic within; nor could any dissection
of it so fail to curl all its living petals
into some inelastic silk-pose;
nor should we speak dysrhythmically,
as though to impose, the fond attires

of our prickliest prose: the faddist's
work, of in-styled clothes—
as if any budding Goddess would unfurl
at the aphonic flourish of warp-strings,
and display unabashedly before the sun,
in gauzy anthesis, her crinoline skin,
crepe-thin, to be torn at the darning wince
of her lover's once-expiring sting!

The Music

With throat cocked, thrush-full, no Cleopatric
word arriving to fret a musing's line, the
musician sets down his timbal and defines
the rest of sound, wherein composites *He*, as Earth
for garth of his bounds, a zoetropic trundle
sent down a slumping ghyll:
                                There is a whine
to thinking that hasn't got a groove: its stature's
like a singeing, whirr that nerves against its clue;
or the mosquito, impinging, with blip-winged purr,
for the hummer's whizzing curve, across the ear,
half-heard—
                 That's what it is—a bird passing
clear of the drum—the fool song of life, bucking
John's sop harmonium, is nested to an inner rhyme—
but's only sound summed, hot eluent chimed
from left to right, as we resolve again, in sore cells
of strained abuse, to seek a slur that sweetly binds
our time to what's so silkenly untrue.

Impromptu #2 (On a Deck)

So it's set: if life's a stage
then we're expected to be
models, through our posturing
Questions, over hardwood, where
fumbled, we've, our latest
foot-lit scene...

                                                                    Not as

here, on a deck,
where blue ripples reprieve
the curtain's last velvet (and
fast-crumpling) screen, if
I'm, for someone,
seen:

                                                                     Not as

a biblic Adam, to stick his red
Race squarely to me; nor any quantum-atom,
to give up all Face, apparently for lease; nor
this whole deep pool's subverse, as some
credible Universe I'd've believed, if
I only had the complete anonymity
to leap—

                                                                    But as

thee, a moving-figure, who at a wrist-
snap's surcease and sideways glance
from the cap of an away-team,
is come to trap whatever's left of me
with doubled words really spoken
into the abstrusion of this scene:
Do you mind if I cast here?—

                                                                    Such that

by one voice's poor reed,
I would unmask all vaunted apostrophes
for the rough hand of a groping—
some chanceful hoping!—and final
re-direction of Me:
Could I cast free?
As each, together!
At your casting, I find the perfect
annihilation of my abused
celebrity—

Evolution

Self, the measure of desire, of
where I want to go and who
I want to be, is heir
of any August morning: its duck
feather, caught by cattail,
flutters in soft wind's rise—easy
to float somewhere, easy to be;
that knows if time will
pulverize, undo the protein,
whose synthesis, made up to lift,
only catches air.

A March Breeze

Heavy in the afternoon made
of time, I find the flowers
of the honeysuckle vine: some
elixir fills this open store of cold,
first fair of spring: it's twisted in
the breeze that's circulating
about my flowing hair. Already
the bees—being thirsty—yet to take
share, form clusters in the sweetened
air, where sounds of industry unborn
ride invisibly this new sort of light
that vends them: as from afar our future
star, undetectable to estranged sight,
lends its weight to yet-worn colors
and bounds—enations, all, I've found,
are enations, all around—like a milder
sound that bends radios inward.
For all of Summer's *to-Be* is pre-tasted
in this slightest of breeze, wherein the waste
of winter, if by a naked shrub I in-breathe
what perfume it secretes, as the fullness
of its time is loaned in un-shown aromas
that resign my merchant eyes at once to defeat—
and becomes a balm to even the coldest
afternoon's heady retreat.

Amaranth

In stubble at the ruderal,
blow-seed sign to go-cross, pride
of soiled asphalt, plastic bag cinctures,
a used chemical jab, and the butt's end-cinders,
is the amaranth, whose stale crown
underfoot gives way to the ugly
and millenary whisper
that follows at a boot's weight—
to a tone with my vacant-lot gait—
the name for what plainly is
trash: *Thus I've come* to not
you know, as it's (often) love
that comes last, but find that
some light is beautiful
whether on this side
or the other
of this alley field, where scooping
up seeds, like rosary—the chaffy
weed-stuff is life
to any one—are
the smaller rats.

Note: Amaranth is a common weed of waste places and fallow agricultural fields; its seeds are nutritious.

To a Bark Beetle Passing My Sight

Go-by! Black Bug, who cuts a-cross
the turned-double saw sky—shove some
of your *one-two!-one-two!* straight through
me: by sum of that recursive three! what eternally
reverses the hard handle of your blighting's
sawn trees—and leaves all biding to a-curse
time! For you are a wrong sign, out-guiding
my ivories: there-by my full forests weep yards
at your rounds, your sleight-of-wing cropping them
out of the light range of day, with chops up-and-down
to scale: your factory of Must, and worm-deep
galleries of sleeping in-laid, all to ground them
to a-dust, by dint of your eclipsing wings' Blade.
Better your a-parting flight should state: "To a-death
is my motion," and have occurrency cup you,
Black Bug, in the notion you mis-staked
as the sky's a-rounding frame: that what a-waits
behind, once your *What*'s left behind, the strobing
body, is to me, whatever the blue's exclosure
tries to a-lign most openly—because it's keeping
us allies *everywhere!*—to a-now that you aren't, Bug,
and are caught: it's not in-stock inside your click-
winged park, dead lumberyard, where sticks roped
under pitched tarps lie rotting (a-stead of holing
pokes into your night-warp), and chain-linked, like
so many of our stopped hearts—Yes, go-by,
You, Precept-ability! For if my forest's no more to be
than a-beam in the wake of your aliasing
black wings, you're a-gone, done in the dark
passing of your passing's by-gone:
and all mine, you Bug.

After a Waxwing Passing Overhead

Like a feathered cross, sometimes
larger than an airplane, sometimes
not, with arcings unaligned
to the windings of a clock, or symmetric
rhyme, the waxwing darts its gold-
dipped plume above mine:
Effortless like a song, sounding
an iced-over pond that awaits
the dream of speech, its cross
drives the inversion, that a tailspinning
swerve completes, before my blue symbol
eyes, shoring what long confusion
the expectant word would, asserting,
repeat. No charity amounts to us knowing
ourselves here, where crowds of mute swallows
tweet out messages of disheartening:
There is no solitude in this, nor in any latitude
of the world, and so on none have I relied,
as you fold your wing to be lifted, or dive,
aboard this soft Apocalypse, down
in the mouth, anointing no silence, nor
to ferry one south, as some far pearl
of sound—that carries-on: You! the last
of all to lay your line upon land,
as you give to me, a man, what
your Highest commands:
Bird of nothing sing
the word that burns a god
deeper than I can understand.

A Prayer II

In every motion a dying—
O Spirit—
that to catch by ration's cold
is to detach a waterfall and hold
it up for a thousand droplets told, line for line,
but never come to talk its fluent course:
Was I thus born to jab cheap holes
by columned speech of a winter's gloss, or
to sweep my hand across, hot palm to thaw
its frozen source? I, who am not become
in gelid stares alone, but am first of sun,
created pair, the warm-feeling—co-heir, who
by rare creation, seals truth, co-aspirant to
a god in me who frees
the world to move.

The Net

Lactic, the sympathic end outstripping
sight, I feature a log-piece and sample
its delights, unblending the ranked forest
from its plumaged hide: Great Real,—
You Jungle!—by what debride, or hollow,
has this star spelunked, unpinned
of your atomy divide? Four wings,
clipped from sticks' morass, are pasted
here, by slim eclose, bat-tenoned
to a stippled eyelash: this fittest of jewels
has come to rest upon my knee!
No prevaricating! At its chance, I summon:
See! (my treasured weapon, tied-to-me)—
Now at it, Net! Go fling! your fine meshing
over this flutter's open get, to taste
by savage pleasure, the irid savor of
banded hues light-sent—But sunning there!
The Dumb Bug, thermizing, in perfect sextuple
aloof, extends its coil, spinel line,
sucking up sweets sun-dried, what metal's
impenetrable, perpetually to my muse.

Memories of a Root-Gatherer

If I saw the summer seek to die
beneath September-solemn tidings—
heavy smokes of gray that once spoke
of heavy harvests—then I would run
as light as a cricket's drum into the thickest
forest, plunge by golden leaves, to shove
little sparks below each gravel-stone
and whisper to the apple and stolid oak tree:
"Look again to the seed."

For the true root follows its own how-to,
if by dark the darkness grows it;
as the retiring soul runs emptier till
it learns to pour its own absence like
a faucet, so the brightest blossom opens
from the core, if for its source it holds
a winter to its will, or the time
when frost is honest:

For when the heat has strayed,
and a decay's upon us,
our voices yearn to speak
of eternal things, of the bud
that blooms in darkest onyx:
constellations in the after-light,
of a Father long-forgotten, or a
Lover unlaid (or at least unwed),
as all jade and purple corollas
fade of blood-dry annulments—

"Yet there is still a treasure here," I say,
as I train my ear to the candle flames

when they twist in molten faces, and listen
for the distant strain of voices naming heresies,
to decipher the insane coordinates:

"Around the hour of the moon,
hold fast to the horn of Horus;
once pass the gates of the Demi-Lune,
and twice-call her dark auroras:
then if, with neither string nor ball,
you can walk straight through
the maze of blazing Taurus,
there inwards-take the revolving Door
of the Gentler One, who waits upon a fount
of soil: Here, *by fallen fruit and tuft*
of green, dig once more the Deeping Root
that reaches through all-rot to breach
the forb that bore us."

And each of us begins
in breathing: the pye-weed,
the pickerel, and the frailest bluet;
for by the heart, or by the fang—*Fear!*—
this ageless art, you knew it: *We* are the way
light expires to illumine, in the one
heave in, and with the one
heave losing; by eyeless magic,
or like its softest proving—the vernal rains
that once lavished us in youth—
we are released, to fall again, as each
inseparate, plashing *Poof!*—
onto the brightly sprouting Earth: like tears
shed for grief's soothing, we are the over-pour
down to the roots below, deeply-moving…

As once, a long time ago, I heard the Good News speak to our renewing:

"Each one, slight sway of approving"

To a Grebe

Holding up to life, in palms small, this
bird of nothing reaches by its fall-
ing into prey: as if torn from the placid
safety of this lake, it dives, under-reaching,
beyond the hard shadows of my eyes, and gulps
what mud mixes with the water of its wake:
At least one aubade—for two—
in this morning, me with you,
I plead, before the plainness of day
spreads out, spans us round, elapses body
into hollow reed—as sense, the contingent
nervosity. Together, we'd speed by oiled
plumes to our abasement, swim past
full nectaries, bee-drooped, and out-mast
the blue's lapped forgery, crooning our
One-song: *Purgation!* of night's Full-Extreme,
that forces eyes to, at a loss, see
a parent sun that laves the cattails
and makes them steam, burns dew
and raises hearts spent in audible
belief to the immortal, honest breeze
of salt.

A Prayer

Like a leaf—O God—
at finial hour, I kneel,
ascend, full-turned to your power,
on limbs laid out, for feeling—All Life—
Astonishment, revealing, my wide
Autumn—Your Color—yet concealing
how the wind is for today
not a contrast if I'm at last
cast into your facing, a blade's forehead*
upon the Earth.

---

*Believers, whether of the Lord or of the Beast, were marked on the forehead.

With Herons

For which the heron declines
its head, the book of the reeds
lies open, plain-spread: in crosshatches of goose,
and piper's tread, lineal marks impress
upon the sand's miscible bed, where light
is blind at times of morning: and leaves—
all meaning to the evacuated mist!
From sun-dewed irises, invisible, carnivorous,
blooms inductively the fish's carcass afresh
to our late supper's on-set: for you, and I,—
we have shared of that silence, well-read
the resurrection of its dead,
so that I, with my history, and you
with your savage dart of blue,
may write into such waters these
few turbid rings of truth.

Lepidoptera

Inform me!—vein-black butterfly—
Bring end to but-life: light's quick hand struts
a scalar trill down your doubled tail
of crypted gold, then accounts, "For-me-not!"
But it's your skipped avatar, which fought
cruel Earth, what chose-to-be, that's just dumb-
dropped, like a knot of autist solidity, to dement
with truant hues my former's hoarder Eye!
When such a turn's more certain to the head
and not the heart—scamps both—I should
ally my lashes to whatever opens up
at the flashing of your bright-mottled lutz,
and twice catch in irid plexus that alighting
fast-brushed: For you to play in form, I draw on
those bolder glasses, flush... and mind what happens!
By some brief Dagger—not of sight, the black-
beggar—you return *in me*, as in specter,
no hollow insect I'd once summed to duel
by lonest pleasure, but a view to newer flights,
my truest vector!

Firefly Jar

in grass, unscrewed,
the firefly lid
falls, loosed.
by dark, kid laughter
becomes abstruse;—
who's to guess
the games to be played
at next year's afternoons:
"All here come clear!" call
Hide and Seek together
from unlaced shoes
running out of August's
rooms.

how a jar
brim's empty, full glow
shed of glass
comes to lose, sole-
winking, some bright
and wider moon
for the stray body's flash—
and drift toward that darker noon—
the sore wing did
phosphoresce, vain,
then renewed, in a blinking,
the yellow link
uplifting
to black leaves—
subsumed.

Faun

For how many twayblade afternoons
have I laid here, and partook, prone
as an incumbent Christ, jaw unhooked,
the whole body, of wafer-Junes—
mouth of Sun, chin trickling-full dew—
by some fallow plot, under cumuloid blue,
fatting on the light and ridden over
with mosquitoes?
If this you call a sacrament,
then it must be the laxest
of all—no pyramid, priest, nor crook'd
blade to release a throat's easy drawl
into Earth's Kentucky bluegrass
chacmool: *Swish. Swish.*—
That's the sound of my legs
crossing and un-crossing beside
the rows of peaking sheaves,
as I peel a cane of grass to inhale
its irredeemable odor: I am
as divine, like this—no mower.

Stone

I've gone further than the trees;
once I told the sun
there wasn't any need
to rise: for Night's divine!
(and in time, a fine murderess...)
Now owls fly fevered
forever shrieking as I roam
devoutly through my alteriorness...

There is an unbroken stone in the river
that talks to me always
about the time it keeps inside itself
hidden, though for what or for whom
it won't say, unless by time it's self-bitten...
But I think I've begun to see-in:
Whatever you call mind, that shape is the shape
of doubt, and always out-going, like the river
itself—the first to empty
wide of the mouth:

To give everything away
doesn't make you humble;
To stop thinking
doesn't make you wise;
You might learn for your living,
but you have to earn
the way to die.

The Story

(interlude)*

*The following four pages are to be read holistically: the verso and recto pages should be seen as a single unit, the four pages thus constituting a single "map" of verbal cont(in)ents perceived in simultaneous "rotation."

"The wind?—It doesn't remember;
nor do the trees. The sun isn't
listening, the flowers don't job
Eves: everywhere the gravities
of things beach into each other;
for each's an orbit set at sea
by softer motions, yet unseen."

"THERE It lies!"

                                                    (yet no *where*

>   —Tell me again the story,
>   of how this brown leaf came to be
>   here by this curving root and tuft
>   of mossy green: *Tell it to me
>   from the beginning...*

When I watch
the wind upon the lake
make its sudden geometries
I do perceive that *this too*
is a circuitry, calculus, and branch
of being, that I know does
not deceive: it exists for itself, is
of itself complete—the wind
over the water is not an act of,
nor any solution to, my misbelief.
That I, sitting by this lake, dry,
await the Story to arrive
composed, by some chance
opening of a throat, exposes
how doped I am to that hopeful
Equator—gaseous body blown
into its most outward crater—who'd so
rudely belabored, with the turquoise poise
of some turvy Uranus:

is it remembered)

How it came

Where a flower is still a flower,
and a leaf is still a leaf,
the trees will not surrender
the meaning of what's green
when it's only something they give
without requirement of receipt:
thus all planets are rounded off
at their ends by no orbit's strict decree,
that a brown leaf might bend
back into a tree's ongoing increase.

All at once along this path,
light's way of flowers and leaves,
orby sights grown to the high expanse
of two pillaring trees that once
spanned a whole star-bound galaxy
that I had failed to perceive
as I went on my walking (too blind
or too fast) through a spider's
web wound, doubly within
and without me, and so impaired
an entire universe with
a single tap of my feet.

Waxwings (for John Shade)

I pick up a book; in a week or two
I will put it down for the last time.
Rarely do I ever read one twice;
it's not the truth that I'm after
but the sound of it:
not to keep *seeing* One,
but to learn to look around It:

Like the sun as it rises, defining today,
present and recognized:
I know with my open eyes
that I am aware, I'm seeking.

Say what you will
there aren't any words for that:
we only ask of names to give up
our weak reading, to lay us over
neatly, a beau's polite sweater,
the puddle of ooze composed of hearts
done in by the call of high-letters:

Today, dead waxwings
again below the window frames.
We picked them out of the bushes like roses.
I'm sure it's no fault of sight that leads them,
as it's not for light to teach in
how to read by any reason: the universe
mirror's on itself, goes on itself in-creasing
and nobody's kept from its illusion alive
through the panes of self's defeating.

Birds

Let's agree it is a bird.
If you've ever been told to look closely
for feathers, all you'll see
is what something is:
If you see yellow, it's finches;
if catbird, coal grays: See
how that one's coated over in polka-
dot arrays? That's just camo for those
that like to stray into the willow's
twixt rays, or for ones that silently wade
through swamps, bent low, always in wait,
to raid at dark from the quakings
of the cattail charades;—
                              Well, that's funny—
Funny, how I can't see anything anymore
by my prized binoculars: it's just blue,
endless blue that lenses fail to magnify.
So when ever I thought I did find a feather,
I didn't really, as no one actually finds
the sky; but we're told it exists, because
the birds—as sure as I—are seen to fly
wherever it's not, because they exist
also. So let's call it a bird
because of course we know that that's
what it is, though (you'll deny)
what it really is, is
what's in front of the sky.

The Filicide

That I pause to sit and write
a requiem for our time's end—that is,
the world I would have said
I threw away, by living alone,
with my sorrowed life, so-feeling,
and so seeing time only furthering go...
—Yet I harvest them! Ripe fruits
prepared of that austerity, those
sugared lures that mined a con-cavity:
I nearly hollowed my whole self,
devouring the drill, to crown a moratorium
over all I thought I could fill with believing
If I suffer, I will...

And how lately have I, too, spoken?
I didn't keep the heart to kill,
though I've watched the good tidings
spill over the land, harrowing the faces
I thought would gaze forever
until... until...
Time defers us, yet turns us to account,
when we move from a seminal disturbance
to the head of a white crowd,
an Isaac of certainty
upon the table of doubt:
As their eyes were watching
for the first race of blood
more devout...

So I turned to my father
to tell him, "If now's the time,
you'd do it right"

so to watch without love
how the body tenses,
unsure of where to land
the first stroke: What is the rite,
Which the correct god to invoke?
But the silent faces could only
glisten, dripping with unease,
to watch their leader falter,
and all his world recede...

Death of Helen

You're right.
So am I.
I nail me;
You deign to cry.

Un-knight me,
I dethrone:
Slave of day-to-day,
picking at a fishbone—

Queen said *nuh-uh,*
Just like mom;
"Flooding breastmilk"?—
That's so glyptodon.

Young, flipping a forelock—
Would'ya love to hoof?—
Tongue-*cum*-heatheness,
leal Finder of roots:

If Loving isn't lingual,
then all I took for Word
was a mad horn piercing
some silence you verbed.

Crest

Make way! If before one, Purple sends her
soft alarm to drive a dream-king's comedown,
and over-slide the lid of some climbing star:
Struggle, cross, a sign—O Sun! what bounds,
Your light foretells—and is—we are.

Miles, miles over log roads, below weathers,
long gone: grave these limits, wronged,
braking a beat-up Eclipse at the black wings
of a throng that glyphs above, retreating
senselessly on and on and on...

Into mists, cold mists of those lower sloughs,
that I drove, half-asleep...—when *she moved*
like an animal, still nude among the greens,
at a sudden appeal to become one

of the wordless ones, like a moon struck
by the placement of things within
her courtesies, what torn purples must cede
to a crest of molten gold.

A Christ-shaped sun in the deep
hollow of my nothing;—
and like the shaking of trees, leaves
when they come to rest
in the blueness of night,
is my entire body laid into calm,
a single wave among the reeds:
a land receiving
the beauty of my mind
astonished by its saturation
into these deserted sands,
always losing,
because they don't know what it means
to hold something.

Last Goose on the Strand

The winter will be hard,
for now I am alone.

This little wing of mine,
it broke; it doesn't move right:
when I run along the sand, I flap,
but it won't hold the weight
of flight, so I have stayed here
in common sight upon
this Autumn pond, sighing when
I float along, and as I drift,
as though in silent song, I lift
my tearful eyes into the sky
to seek where my flock
has flown:
I—

Have never known a name
to ask of mercy, never been
shown the reason to pray,
but I *do* know how the sun goes,
and I *do* know the turn of days:
they're the quern of my body
and the anguish that grinds me
like a mill: you see, there are gods
that dwell inside of me still,
who keep on this yearning,
most ageless vigil: gods
of wind, gods of rain, gods
of stars, of leaves and lakes,
and at times—it's true!—

I feel them wake: a pain, I believe,
that even *you* once knew: and yes,
there's one of sky, too:
I feel him in my heart and in
my broken wing, this crooked,
useless thing that keeps me
grounded here, nibbling weeds, small
seeds, the gall of familiar things.
And I am well fed.

But I have dreams.
Some nights, I have seen
a crystalline country where long lakes
sparkle in the clean, unbreaking light
of a southerly plain, where
my brothers and sisters glide
in the perfect sun and in the morning
rain, and I get along with them
and we're simple together, unafraid...
We glide, and we flap and we circle
in our play, while the lilypads glisten,
and the flowers murmur of bees
all through the undying day...

And then I found
upon my waking,
all that I craved but never minded
for long desire and fitful dream
was here—and had always been—
here, beside me, in between the scattered
down and stinking feces: the lake,
gossamers threading the cattails
by two; the blossom, upon its sun-hit hour,
in opalline drops of dew; except—

my heart!—
there were *none* of you:
for you have gone far,
far away, beyond the skies...
And it's always at this sorrowing thought
that I start to cry as I drift,
and I start to drift as I cry...

But there's a whisper in the goldenrod,
that tells my heart's drunk overlong
of thistle-cups steeped in dew: for when
the night hums with different voices
and it's a colder wind that runs the willows
through, by such signs as these
I begin to remember that I once knew
what all the crickets and the asters
told to their lovers in the grasses,
when the body ceased to move:

"When we've come to love,
we come to turn us each into
the one wing that sweeps us
up into the senseless Blue."

But still the winter will be hard
on me, for now my wing
is bended: yet if I'm at last
to stand this shore alone,
may I be enough

to match
the sun

ascendant

Obit

Stung! Like my heart
around a crucifix becomes;
by the one, true thump—*a-tum!*—
that charged me from that moment on:
Yes, *you*—
the golden man, shocking light,
who came of my darkness, full caress
to cross all the blight, insanity,
and gave me some sight, more or less complete
that I thought I could keep—by what right?—
or take-hold: How dumb to believe I was
somehow bound for that winning!
When I was only caught, a bound spider wearily
spinning again and again its bled-white catacomb:
All miracles we call miracles
are really circles whose ends
weren't pulled from our threads; yet,
if we're one miracle—you mean, so it's *true*?—
that it does come,
is in the breaking perfect
circle we spun
out of You.

The Cross of My Heart

A dark wing tears
the villous air of my wide
and open body; the moon hangs low
to the west, its angel smirk's
a light hurled through the blackwork
of trees: it's all cuts and bruises out here,
where the beaten sky's my blood transfusion
through the vining neural branch,
as many thoughts find in me
their chance at death:

>Devour, then repent,
>and devour again.

Don't hold the weight of all your words.
If you listen close while walking
the street at night you can hear
the sound of a rat cage shuddering
in the corner of an apartment room.
I hear it for the last time. Go.
Door thud, lock click.

How I wanted to be opened!
How I only bled instead!
The cross of my heart is the torment
I am destined to know.
I *think* that I'm with love.
But no:—
The wing is not too heavy for this flight—

>*Whatever I say, I've sold—*

and the cross of my heart
receives another Christ.

Tree *after Annie Dillard*

sap's running—
sap's made to-tree—is
formlessness, outpouring:
the liquid funnel
reaching through twig,
root-cap, xylem,
each unfolding leaf:
a tree-giving form
(that mixes in sweets)
is sap-moving
through space; when
in open, is free—
then in-closing,
secretes:
a vessel
that fills itself
up with emptiness
the light

Easter

       Go sane Girl, and send away
       the angels; they have no authority
       to speak of what they do not know.
       I've no need of the bleached pinion;
       such pets confuse for pretty conception
       what comes naturally by earthly perfection—
       But *you* know this: You, who stand
       with a patient hand gripped to the lip
       of my cave, cold lichened clay—do you recall
       that sad crumbling phrase?—and choose
       for your chapel the nothing
       my Word had failed to name.
       You are that foretold one, the comfort
       for which they pray: Go! and bid them
       gently, by a master's hand, gently,
       gently along your way.

            —Please, mister, won't you come talk
            to my dead brother and tell him a story?

            —Child, it's true I once knew the way
            to call him, but I don't think in stories
            anymore. He has been sleeping for only
            a little while. Go. It takes only your touch
            to wake him.

I close another botanist's journal—
the names mean nothing to me anymore—
as I muse on the lawfulness and the poison
of the naming of the flowers:
Once, I too passed in the garden,
and caused the swollen buds to open

for beetles who ate them raw—
there's no haven, ultimately, for lilies,
no place where they stay unflawed.
So I let the winter turn, and forbade
the servants to inurn the petals
spent in Earth, nor adjudge the beauty
of its Laws, for there will come again a blossom
to draw from soil the depth of light before all:

> *Come spade, you're wedded to it, as am I*
> *to your thrust; the flowers of Love*
> *will rise of us, for by blood we are kept*
> *to that trust: This is the furrow*
> *and the flesh is to fill it, a loss for all loss.*
> *I am come to lay myself into your moss;*
> *the only creation I claim was not my own.*
> *My word is now yours to sow.*
> *Did I not say that Love*
> *is death in Truth?*

On the third day
I washed my own feet and afterwards
let him touch my breast

Amen Corner

the sweet clover yawning leaves
a Buddha's wing among the twining
wreaths of virgin's bower and cinquefoil,
where all florets nod to neverminding

the fable that night coiled: if caught
for a web of silver strung out like a cable
of light, as it threads the hazing line,
she spreads, upon the table, unkempt,

of apostlry and vine, where the crow-dark
suspends in sorrow's nimiety of fronds,
for none but the day's moth-quiet applause,
one long pliant skein of crepuscular hue:

no braid of a serving-maid, nor gauze
of a serpent chanteuse, high ward
of the Egyptian papoose: be it a spider,
a shrug, white spire of blooms.

New Lexicon

A poem is leading us there.
The branch of desire is no apothecary's
trick; I have all of my organs
mapped, and yet I still can't tell you
how to translate the heart's tick:
Listen, this second's
silence has got to count
for something, or else we're nothing
but contrapposto torsos forever making no motion,
like blind Venuses strolling blithely without
an inner ocean: the obscurity in skin
is reified at the itinerant's
touch: no moonlight is so
silky, no river bends so much
as this body; my hand has foreknowledge
of your naked stomach, is practiced
in your smoothed ampoule:
Grace is *held* in someone near—is a droplet
compelled, this tear—
I do not believe it is something
autoclaved, pipetted, or electrophoretically
smeared by a hand above; it is made
in the shudder of two loves
from whatever heaven is cleft
wide enough to receive
a leader's cry.

Yes, Love

The way to Love
is in seeking without
leading the mind to a needing;
is in all things a heeding
of no Thing-in-all, but of all-beating
hearts, that by one heart's defeating,
finds Love takes no single part of anything at all;
like how, at the first dews of my call,
a slate-dove was led to my lips, but sipped
for its sound-ness, fled as the gibbon tongue
howled out in loon-strangeness:
for no thing loves less its name
but love's what proves it nameless:
How no call is all of *You*, your inaudible undressing,
as Love's *No* inheres in Both, our naked *Yes-sing*:
"Yes" with mouths open,
"Yes" with mouths close,
"Yes" with breaths hot, and O—
"Yes" with your wicked kissing...
and "Yes" and "Yes" and "*Yes*"
until the word dissolves
in your body and you walk with it:
Yes to the small hairs
above your upper lip, *Yes*
to the uneven complexion
of your face, *Yes*
to your body weight, *Yes*
to the cry you model
with your rickets-words speech

Bright

bright is the world
      the flux of stars
on the river surface
hide dark below   the charms
of clams and fishes
              shine too I know
if on the sand spits their bodies
might open, guts carved
out by other life, white
skeletons that glisten with
the same magnitude
      as the brightest named
           stars.

Tying the Knot

We're alive to understand.
Some will tell you there is nothing
to understand, and they're right,
but still we have a command
to know the confines of space
the loess of glaciers
the lease of hate
the fate of Evil
at Love's going-rate: your child
in the grass, besides, lifting up
play-blocks—to a new building's rise,
or to arrive at play-time's last stop?
I'll never know the thing you replied
to silence the snake, wringing your hair,
while still wet from the swamp, throat
waterlogged of the despair
that pushes up flowers—for long irises,
benthic, are your powers risen from rot!—
and yet at times I feel
that I do know, have seen it
exposed like buttocks:
known it with your same wincing grin,
neither of shame nor chagrin, but
in a more abject bouquet bundled
up with a sin, that to you, is for giving
all of it, away.

After Rain

When after rain but before it's blue,
and wet's the world, whose neuter Zeus
did furnish for bronze, a spear, what each
spare cloud had sent oddly, sent clear
of a pronoun that ends pure, elided:
the gem, agent of its own throwing,
studs the lake, concentricizes, around
my target's focal *here*: that unreal *I*—
widely-spoken—if sown for its out-flowing,
most Indian tear, once chosen, now grows
of that more unknowing: *Fear*—my sublime
emblem—or flagging wheel now set to
its rolling, as by a-going, wave-smoothed,
into life's new, apparent just-so-ing.

To the Newly Sprouted

Stripped, as by flood, like cotyledons
on fresh mud, I'm proved, a wet
nude (neither flushed, nor in froth of
faked spume), by perfect indetermination
of waters' intrepid move: for in the suck
of clay, wet mucks, I've assumed
a sure shoot, at the bless of an impress,
horned hoof, or paw—the feline prick
of a claw—as one to thwart a sycamore's
raw rooting, or to make of might's scrawl
a gilt arabic, scripts of light's fall below
the coursing, like fluent law: where above
the jointed skimmer jots its hurried trace
to place in anchorage, by-way
of any race's brook, run, or rill—Hereby
the slightest of tilts! tug-of-earth,
I span this dry surface, snake a name
across the curving shore, braving one
blossom, sans surety, before an ocean's
fossorial reward.

(along Furnace Run, circa 2:00 in the afternoon)

Laughter

I cannot keep the yellow flower, growing rare
among the waving rushes—flowing where
they've wrung of squirmy peat, a way to stand
above the reek—from crying out, as with me,
the deeper measure of all-surrounding's
three: the sandpiper, nudging his crook
among the flats; the fish's wet and sordid
gasp, to bound, at a quarter-eighth, another
lake he can't a-ground (but for the four
fragile wings he just, sinking, ate); and the
pondlily's antennal eye, jaundiced at life,
to eat out a light from the unscalable
blue of a June-day's sky—So
nothing staves us! For all our crimes,
the murky cycles of hunger, with jealous
hooks, we catch at a weird allozyme:
Nothing.
Though I would wait a century
to flick an eyelid, millennia to curl
the corner-lip: for what is face but
a place to smirk an eon, a treble
nebula to shake the slow waste,
as endless endless echoes jolt
into a silver clefture's shape?
For we are the bodies, bodies of time
connotively condensed, to grumble at
our score of breath, grand extra-orchestration
we mistake as the grave-clatter of our death...
But does the Ever never sate, or seek to
hear us further out—maybe to, at last,
us out?—from the dark of God's good-gracious

Mouth, being-ceaseless, in-harmonic, that
keeps us crying doubt, like the completelessness
of the flower, yellowing there, there
above the livelong rushes, that I wonderfully
feel as me, is me, and not unconscious?—
Though of course I couldn't be, no more
than the saliva of a chewing insect
mixes its entirety with the leaves', or the fugal
heat of a goose's fecal tract, emptied elsewhere
along the beach, transpires the fire that's inflected
through a waiting seed; though maybe—someday,
God grant me—I'll be the last to play the parting
of these teeth, when by a hooking line,
long cast (and repeat), I greet the scission
of a godlike grin secretly caught laughing
itself as me!

To a Young Fisherman without a Pole

How's it done? If not by your pre-pube tug
under a blue ball cap, un-reeled to
any hooking: so love's recreant
dreams of his out-cast, that, without
rigging, catches, by the trillion,
bigger brook-fishes untrammeled
by our Finder's triple fleet;—
not that my afferent rite could train you
to the tracing of the high magnetic
stars, nor aright the tilted crowns
of a thousand tarred-up pines,
that ply the forest-waves of the night!—
s'what I lucked, too, my boy,
in those years of all-spite; now,
I'd task them, 'f I were you, 'less
your cargo's fooled of dim treasures,
how one instead endeavors to trust
inside the coffers of the heart, self-
broken: lone pier where ships emboldened
most fear to embark, for hot palms
shelled 'round clear opals stolen
of the dark: Love's rawness!—
Now you: Keep-to! Keep-to!
that threadless wrist-snapping!
Keep throwing out your wishes,
faked mayfly always returning guts-empty.
I know what lake's fine nets abide yet
low enough to receive, with big-eye pupil,
that unpronounceable humility
to float, as the loose discarded string
of some old alexandrine
coils about a drifting reed,

permitting all indifference
to your catching.

Cultivars

When we were children,
we tore the blossoms from the bushes
in the garden and cried, pointing
at the blood stretching from
the clenched bouquet,
until our mothers hastened
from screen doors with bandages
smelling of antiseptics:
Do you remember when sweetness
was as simple as a kiss
over our torn fingers, if we promised
not to repeat on this, and keep
what our hands held first
before the flowers stolen?

I propose the animal rose
knew rightly the full honors of the heart;
and grew on, when nightly, for long hours,
I pulled all the charts, stalked lines over maps,
to mine of blacker forbs one drop
at last of that awful red ore, which
a petalled tongue could lick fast
at its quick, and lawless grasp: *I'm stung*!
and so the bled word runs, sprung of that quiver,
one gasp to the heart which no cherub
delivers, but's flung straight through
the whole, by death's plucky finger:
"*Enough!* of all untorn living—
Fear is the sharpest way
to acquire a life worth
a giving."

Was it you, then, or me—
the first, I mean,—
to breed the rose which has no thorn?
By what loss of childish courage
do we deny ourselves her savages
for which into love we are born?
Now our fear is the same as our neutral living
for blood is hard to come by
the fix of silicon chips and sitting, when
it's only by the prickle—our divine blood letting—
that we are led into her resolve, for giving:

We were wrong, we admit it.

She awaits now the Apology.

We only ever wanted to know we bleed.

Impromptu #3 (In the Garden)

"Wither more and more, black Chrysalid! thou dost but give the winged beauty time to mature its splendors."
                                                            Margaret Fuller

—*That's* the eclose (and the double
fold), the wings that earn the worm its grave,
for the still-born star is bound to beam:
as each one seeks to innervate the Eternal Ray!—
and the chrysalid's alike to those slender braids
of the moon, what she spools nightly
from cold-lit streams, an imperial lace, by which
she weaves into flight's shaping,
the boneless bird of four wings
that flies for no eye, but darts farther up—
and larks away! at the sharp measure
of an eager-cock's crow, who shakes
my garden's droopingest blades: for each
beady droplet that twinkles then rolls precipitously
down into the clay, excites my errant sight
to run clear out of love, and thus I haven't come
close enough to hear the parent hum of *what it is*
which vibrates within those budding strings, that
his crowing twanged: some chanticleer tug!
of one bird's summary disclaim: *I'm me!*—
whose ardent strain and echoing reveille
overlays the ruddied haze, smoking purples,
and heavy fogs that clog the destined wings
of so many white-sleeping and devoutly dreaming
things, spun all together inside night's close-knit
seams...
                                That unravel

like the blackbirds do, 'on dawn—a shadow
sifted—as the veery eyeball of the sun
lifts its fiery lid to look steadily upon its native
throng: proud robins busily disgorging meals
to their nest-full mobs; or weary crickets,
who fritter away each summer day in our lawns,
their prating chirps like filler to all this choral song,
that throbs, light-come and light-gone, to cudgel
whatever's grown solid of Love's coursing blood,
sweeting sinews, and mud-marrowed bone:
All her vast, brutal, beating body of drone!
Earth's vessels and vital gristle, whortling stars,
and core, burning us—Oh!
                                       Burning, Burning us, so—
to grant us this quickening, of our new-crinkled
wings—as the fluids flow—soon to lift us
kindly into trees—or into quicker beaks?—who'd
untimely rip us, our falling scales to aimlessly blow
among the old bars of a song that knows of
no-close—
                That's always harping *Yes!* (when it's
always darkening: *Oh No!*)—or that's at best
Oh-Yes! precisely *when* it's *All-No!*?—
                                    Oh, however it's so—
For I've only ever held onto this one hope:
to come close enough to kiss you, and taste
the poisoned nerve of the dying bird that
parts the full lips of day: *Everything* (and
this I heard, for good) is what's divisible,
and I can only love it that way: your skin,
the bramble, a spider leg: each lends to each
its one, and finest tissue, once I've lost
the larva's mind to crave, and raises us,

by triumph of any over one, on wings
from that twice-flown song: *O Say!* —
to what, after all, two *can't* say—
and thus makes our livable, and most possible,
break away—

The Path

> *"The way up is the way down."*
> Heraclitus

First, dark: foot-shuffling through duff,
flushing critters from shinleaf and clumped moss,
while knocking for fairies on old stumps
(either of ash or the Skull's tree-husk): just
a few earwigs and bum moths.—Then, next,
at the boot's-taking, the mind races, up-straining
through vapors, at black trees tapering up, up,
and up—into dumb cloud, like Gothic spires:
hooker fingernails raking the sour paunches of God.
Yet none'll scrape the Body's innermost layer.
So dull mists lace over a matins gloom (as the chanted
breath remains forever, unimproved): *No*-way
was desirable, that I knew and couldn't move,
with legs tied to unsoled shoes: *three times*
I heard feral dogs bark, and *twice* morosely
the sleep-owl hoot—

Was it stupid, our Staking's claim?
But his After-All *never came!*
By dread of night we amble, over trails
disused, clueing to cellular optics, when
chancing to find an atman's fuse, kneeling,
we site our campfire right on top it—to light up
another *There* to-go! yet ever more quickly to blow
our proofs on that one bad excuse: *"It's exotic!"*
Or rather, more like *moronic*: 'cause someone
else's *Up There* is no better (after all) than
our dead-promise. For are we not as heirs
of that past prose and typecast Dream?
When it's deemed that believing in vast life's

necrotic, we leave ourselves little expanse
of conceiving the soul's wider tropics—until
we claw outside the stalls of our faux Enlightening,
clear our throats, and call on the brightening
horn of the Moon: whereby night-summons,
we plummet unexpectedly into the sudden
Lunar Combe...

If *hers* is to reach this mountain bald,
then it's a far weedier trail than easily-quailed
foots have installed, when, logging-on to dementia,
we transposed for Venus a few rows of 1's and 0's—
all of the blooming *supposed*, in absentia.
Oh, how we *do* Fall—so low!—
And so let *this* be scrolled:
Whatever belief you're assured of,
she's sure to blow, now fragrantly open,
now closed together under ice-cold,
for the crampon (Full attraction) is hers
to elicit of all eyried *ut-oh*'s...
—Is it Hell, her odors, to oppose?
No more am I certain!
than the path that I chose: to breathe in
her sense most deeply through the *nose*.

(Clingman's Dome, May 2016)

The Meadow

I walk into the meadow
to read the buttercups by Cycle:
as I know this morning's rain is ocean
siphoned up and then out-drained,
like puke upon the dichotomous blades,
inebriated by the proof of night.

I walk into the meadow
to read the buttercups by Vessel:
as strange aurous bodies, twinned
with mystique, if carefully strained
through night's fairy-scrims, like rain
from the anuses of Orphic cherubim.

I walk into the meadow
to read the buttercups by Buttercups:
I almost undo their true name
(or what the dew had clung
to), from what all coruscation conceals,
when by the sun a whole blossom,
in the fifth-then-sixth petal,
is revealed:

I walk into the meadow
and I walk into it again;
I enter the meadow
from a thousand different
entrances: the meadow is
always there, it awaits my return
at every calm hour, in every calm air,

dew wetting the forearm
skin of my up-given limbs
as I stand still by the buttercups
on a windless night.

Mountaineer

I'd climb a mountain
if my paths were uppity,
but mists deem it's clear I was
made to be-low here, so right-here
that I can only *know* here—
Here, here (with small under-fear
that I'd blow it all by my quest-
ing) and not surmount this raisure's
pile of smoked stones, atlassing
an orb—It, Alone—For must I?
If you're the god! and wide-backed—
Thus I've come to see them:
with their Mights and their brutal Math,
those First Come of the mind
trussed to all-graphs, and manic
enough to hard-drive a mountain
(from boil to bust), hoist its bulk
up on a muscled back, and strut
aridly along the tracks of un-probable
beginnings to some pinnacle's
table-end, Twelve-to-one—but it wasn't
that sum! As only that comes—
so I claim!—in between, like slit gleams
from the sitter's winking-eye game.

Sheep

I'm counting sheep
as a marbled Milesian crumbles
from forums out of mind:—
Rain, time, have at those fountains!—
When I'm counting sheep,
the ring and middle finger
feel courses through the humid hairs,
reaching down to heat, body-deep
skin of a heart-beating animal.
Aloof! Most Beautiful Helen;
Aloof! Triple Magi, the Finders;
All aloof! You, praetor Mathematicians,
fine-tuning your proscriptions:

I'm counting on sheep.

Yet I haven't truly counted on—
Would I know how?—
I only do: *"That one and that one,
and Oh! that one, too,"*
meaning nothing more.
No animal amounts to a name, so why
do you trust in the fame of lame theorems?
Nevermind (so never-*kind*!) the proofs
you've done; each insolvent book has only rung up
more service to *your* One—but what if we could
reach that greater Sum, teaching: *By this!*
That so-troubling blemish, *here*?—perhaps
the native tissue, perhaps only a scar;
perhaps it was there to be all along
from the start: *this place* for a palm

to warm the length of a snout—But *woah!*
Don't try to steer, and don't hold! To *learn*
your reach, you've only got to know how to keep
your hand unarmed! For my yarn's only to guide it,
to tell of how one feels a little more divine
by ploughing over the skull and going down
the woolly spine

On The Beach

As a pebble to this sand, admonish me
for believing I was made for more
than your rocking and replacing, rolled
body to a wave-form—for the waters,
lakes, like our mastering, make up
the speech, and rake over saline clumps
of articles, amerous debris, upon
the beach of our destitution, desert
of dust I shake from word repeatedly.

Why's it always that
for every Laud that gets its wrack
along this duning, there's a hole
that predates the dive, like a Hell,
to soften the subside?
I recognize its padded palm
upon the sag bones of my shoulder,
sounding a name I once used before
I finished all forgetting. Did I need
ears, a mind, or time to recall?
When the tide comes, I will chase
crabs between the knotted coral
and feel blood, if it runs.

For Life, known only by its loss—
and Heart, if I'm to become your cross,
then I'm not less than the sandpiper
in its million forms, picking from mud
the stuff of its life among the drift lines.

Highland II (Prayer at Seip Mound)

All of your religions
All of your hymns,
holy sayings, prayers,
and all of your *Hims*—

All of your science
All of your plans
All of this nation's rivers
and all of its dams—

All of your offices
and all of your years—
With all of that money
You could start minting tears—

All of your futures
and all of their exoplanets
All of this payment:
I say you can have it

All

For a face lit by twilight
when the air smooths to blue,
to mount my gaze among stars
by the mark of night's bruise—

For the deer in the meadow
and the bats in the sky:
It doesn't have to be more than this
to soothe the heart's cry.

It doesn't have to be more
than a plea at dark's sign
for I to take Yours
and You to take Mine.

To My Child

A dying child stepped to me and asked
if heaven and hell were real—　　　I said *yes*
they were:
We lived through them, so they existed;
God is no creator, made nothing;
God's synonym
for the creating, the act of, making.
Your breath, your hands:
all divinities, child;
even your tears, child,
your sad falling
tears.

From the creekbed, the meadow,
hands rise;
from the streets, sewer bars
hands prize
you again, shaking
up the blessing—
for it's either by violence or caressing
that makes you the bettor of truth:
So why does it matter, child
if there's blood in our love, child
and love in our blood;
when it's only a tear, my child
falling over soil,
that draws the sunflowers from the darkness
to gape at the sun all day—and tell me
who created *them*, truly,
who did that, my only child,
my little dead one

Next Chapter

Close the page, the book
of the world is opening.
The mist of god will dispel
the gist of the mystery
we nightly are: when our sun's impositioned,
our mouths to a flame, what being
sounds in the stars' infinite collisions
with the darkness of our faith:
that unloving space and its gormless
names to forget, for one better
exchange between those high-stemmed
lights and our unparented relations;
what will lead us through fire
to inform some new kind of cerebration
once all of us *here* are run
on love's full-rotation:
So turn-on now!
A Christ goes back to sleep
and returns the stone to its place.
Who is to walk in our dreams
for another thousand generations?
It is the next one
who reaches into the chest
and places the incepted heart
onto the table; the one who sighs
to say, "It was all for the best, I guess,
so the mind was just a different way to pray,"
—and turns the age.

Truth/Clouds

The truth is
that everybody already knows what the truth is;
that if we'd agree
the first breeze said it perfectly,
then maybe our number-minds
would blow a little storminess from out
our over-fed mouths and form
a front of rainclouds that reign-black:
and by stranger weathers
turn our Ever-Afters into laughs!
Like the formerly-gay rustle of the aspen leaves
and their silvery claps to the wind's
invisible, mesmeric tap-dance: this small
disturbance—it's so simple it's too vast—
for the TV-station bimbos to forecast:

On my surest azure mornings,
I know I am the son of God—
Not *the* Son of God,
but one of the actual ones—
As, stands the sum of my bodies
sedately beside the sun,
I watch the early cirrus run
ornately on sky's rising blue-print:
Some say they fly better satellites
for measuring that tint, which *might,*
if you squint, get it right—
but would I televise it?—No God!—
And why?—'cause it's miracle
enough to try and see pure, as clear
as the Day live-streams the Night!

"Hell, I suppose..." —I know,
I know, that's *your* cloud that
probably westerly blows:
closing up to disaster, as it drowsily scrolls
along, browsing whatever Alleluias
still obtain to the few who haven't refused to love
because it's dark.

The Lilies of the Day

The creation of this day
is a lily and not the stem
to its wish: is a damselfly, a valley,
a nylon cord, a fish; and this morning
is reeling to pull its own death
up in long, silky wisps
from the coldest lake, like any
living thing that thickens
the air with its breath—

And yet it's fair to say
"I *saw* You!" at the light's peeking-through:
by a lake, in this morning's take-
placing, that I saw it all light-speaking
of You—but couldn't *I* show You, too?
How was it that I was never
told the whole-god-ness of dawns,
of thistles, of frogs, but had to earn it
all by my fearing—not by any disappearing,
for it had to near me patiently through
some sunken inner ear, until with time it grew
swollen with Augusts, with dews,
with all the minnows, and all the blues
of my neighbor's fishing eyes: his labors
and private sorrows, as with a long sigh
he casts his ancient line out to the sky
and says at all this hard sight:
"Yet I made love with my life."
And his face softens
after a kind, as he swings his arms again,
and his face begins to look a little more
and a little more like mine.

—That I never could find in the tired looks
of my books, once-opened, untidily strewn
and poor-read: for I'd heard it once-said
that Everything ends up in them to find a white bed
between those hardbound sheets, there to sleep
profoundly by straight-rule: O Pearly Nouns!
of saints, great leaders—all your readers,
so fooled! by those woozy iambs, to dream
the Dream both beautiful and cruel, wherein
one's line is held mindlessly, over a puddle of drool;
while nightly—so long as this life holds—there's
a tussle of linen that twists vitally to compose
the meaning of that one, and sweetest
of all folds: for in the bending of bodies
given to holy in-crease, one reads of the absent sheet
that's turned over, in order to re-pleat what no
graven words would dare to make bold:

that I feel any ordinary day could spread-whole,
given a lily, or spore of green,
spot of mud, a heron croak, or bee
sting: so then you could show it, too,
and drop your stack of sheets, high heaps
of thesauri, to try a new verb that rhymes
only with *You*: how with time and with breath—
all that a master-mind would seek to uproot—
there comes a flopping moment, perhaps immortal,
by the steady grip and up-pull, as the silvering
thing jumps from the pool and sticks
its red tongue to the spool, gasping death,
lips sucking Earth air, life-full.

The First Religion

Somehow born, we—
are our children, are free, minds
right for in-forming—
have never the need to learn Core,
for our currents go on about us, coursing
over all this good green earth
that our child's Ear keeps
hearing, keeps sounding out
clear, never closing, but setting it all down
closely, by *Here*: impressing the fingermarks
deep into our clay-soft dark:
this unfired, untiring, kneading clump
of a heart:

we grow;
the violet shows us
what Spring is,
and our eternal infantility
keeps up the fertile ability
to agree
with all living:
the swerve of an ocean,
a gnat levering frail wings,
a saucer pitched to the floor, broken;
the mystery of any thing—
we call it all into us, when so opened
won't we

go *into* it: we—
are like rootlings,
peach-hair upon pubescent cheek,
as we seek to show it,

with wild eye-lightnings: this tiny chirping
thing, divining the deep sense within
our two cupped and dirty palms, held upwards,
twice-made and perfect as alms, to sturdy adult faces
in sturdy adult calm, who've long
learned how to chew on wishes, gone
cold: "Let go of it, you're getting too old;
it's time to bring the bacon home."

But we hold on
to it, the throb and the itch
it leaves in our palms, and discretely mold it
within the cricks of our skin—some things we're not
told—or fold it into our own vibrant micro-clime,
perhaps like an arcuate finger-line, to imprint
our complicity over all this sordid, ancient crime:
That I remember,
as I was turning to sleep,
someone said lies on our bed
like a sheet, *Tide*-bleached, that
gets borne up when we dream, to adorn
an ageless bird that burns
and returns each night without a mate
for its ashes: that if you've learned all the fun
of climbing rungs above the mind's traffic,
you'll know for every hand that reaches out
to grasp it, there's a foot that's stung
running bare among the buzzing grasses.

Although, I suppose—
what I know, that you know—
We

will have, after all, nothing to show
for it—no ribbon nor reward to attest it;
none for those who flop, hamstrung,
and none for those who run the fastest,
but we loved running all the same,
running
as though no dark could outlast us.

Telling

Had I forgotten
that I cast a shadow
in the moonlight?
I almost did, I did.
That I am still
a solid body
in the darkness
is good to know.
Do you think
other people know
they cast a shadow
in the moonlight?
Should I tell them?

About the author

Dylan Stover has worked variously as a landscaper (from which he developed an acute antipathy to lawnmowers), a donut-maker, a field botanist, a factory assembler, a museum technician, and as a clerk in a cheese shop. Poetry, he is assured, isn't a real job, just a way of speaking. He currently resides in Cuyahoga Falls, Ohio, where he works for money. He doesn't own any pets.

Made in the USA
Middletown, DE
05 August 2023